"Each of us experiences life in our own context, but for all of us there is a struggle to balance the reality of life with our needs and our dreams. Perhaps the most difficult thing of all is to value our life and who we are, and to direct our life in a manner that honors it..."

— Laurie Harper, "A Taste for Life"

Dedication

Mom
• Bob • David • Amy
Ken • Margo • Pat • Alene
Charley • Robin • Cathy • Karen
• Mary • Sylvia • Alice • Roselle
Ginny • Laura • Kay • Joy • JoAnne
Carolyn • Dale • Jack • Jan • Cindy
• Sandi • Bertie • Diana •
Georgiana • Dan • Peter • Paula •
Avis • Judith • Melodie • Joyce •
• Julie • Tom • Kaye • Woesha
Racquel • Dorothy • Elizabeth •
Don • Sharon • Diane • Sarah • Jim
• Jeanne • Leonard • Sandra •
Gene • Joan • Art • Chris • Rose
• Anne • Charlene • Susan • Sheila
John • Deanna • Shou • Sparkle •
• Carol • Jake • Julia • Rafferty
Louisa • Amanda • the people of
the northwest

Love Comes in
Simple Ways

3

Windows' Table of Contents

WINDOWS*

When the present seems hopelessly bogged down I turn, for a few moments, to the future.

I feel an intuitive attraction pulling me. I can see and feel the future. I know where we will travel if we move beyond our current life-patterns.

Crises always precede perceptual transformation. It's as if we need to be bumped into an ability to see clearly.

The choices seem obvious, but you must make the commitment.

connection not elitism
empowerment, not power over others
community not isolation
participation not observation

self-discipline not mellow
touching not sex
intuition as well as logic
humor not hopelessness

grace not control
optimism not pessimism
meaning as well as comfort
spirit not emptiness

Open the window of the future that is within you, peek out, stretch, lean towards it and prepare to tumble through.

* Reprinted from the last page of *Success Is The Quality Of Your Journey*

SIGNPOSTS

Ch'ien/The Creative: "When an individual draws this oracle, it means that success will come to him from the primal depths of the universe and that everything depends upon his seeking his happiness and that of others in one way only, that is, by perserverance in what is good."

— I Ching

This is the day to think about the rebirth, the new year. For me it will be a year of travel, to China, Tibet and elsewhere. It will be a year to travel within and without, a journey toward the heart.

I sometimes call it trekking in the "Inner Cosmos" to lighten my own vulnerability. When we trek about in the depths of inner geography, gentleness and grace are only moments away from anger and pain.

When I started trying to understand years ago, I chose anthropology as one path. I wanted to learn the answers cultures other than my own had chosen. I taught comparative religion, the universal search for ecstasy. I taught cross-cultural morals and values, the search for what is right. What I learned was respect for the God within all living things.

The journey continues. Take a few steps with me in honor of the new year. Choose your own way, listen to your own voices. Pick up guides wherever you can but remember to let go of them so you can keep moving. Remember to take time to rest now and then, to renew your spirit.

Start the new year with your own journey toward the heart. Here are some signposts to light your way. As you travel, remember that we are all connected and that the destination is the same for all of us.

The longest journey begins with a small step and ends with a small step. — Anonymous. Take a step. If you don't like the step you chose, then try another until you find the one that is right for you.

8

I am lovable and capable. Sometimes others remind us that we are worthwhile people. Knowing you are worthwhile from within, mistakes and all, is the best daily reminder.

Self-knowledge is for the purpose of contributing. — Alene Moris. Take time to understand yourself. Self-knowledge is essential if you are to have a quality life.

You are the only one who can take care of your inner child. Are you still looking for the perfect mother or father? Are you still trying to improve the ones you have? Practice taking care of the child within you. Only you can do it right.

Happiness requires action. Happiness requires involvement, interest, commitment and a meaning to our lives beyond ourselves.

Don't confuse kindness with weakness. Gentle people have special strength. Sometimes in others there is only an illusion of strength. Remember this in passion and love.

I am never upset for the reason I think. Check and see if you are afraid of something or angry for some other reason than what you started with.

If I hurt enough, I'll change. Pain is a wonderful and terrible teacher. If you feel tension, confusion, boredom or depression, your body is asking you to change.

Every problem has a gift for you in its hands. — Richard Bach. Wisdom comes from tapping our deepest emotions. It's learned by moving through problems, not by standing still. Use troubles to fine-tune your character.

I cannot control the thoughts and acts of others. Peace of mind requires you to realize you have no control over others. You may want someone to be more thoughtful, but you can't make him.

All you need lies within. — C. Eden. Self-knowledge is sometimes painful and very hard to find. When you do discover something about yourself, it's a wonderful accomplishment.

Love is something you do. Put love into the world and it will come back to you.

Angels can fly because they take themselves lightly. — Jean Cocteau. Try to see the absurdity in life. You deserve to laugh.

This too will pass. Time is healing. All painful things in our past become easier to handle. Feelings don't last forever unless you want them to.

I did the best I could with who I was and what I knew at the time. It is hardest to forgive yourself, even for things that happened long ago. If something is bothering you, make up for it in whatever way is left. Then let it go.

If you want peace you must give up conflict. It's easy to think that conflict (anger, fear, irritation) comes from what someone else is doing to us. Choose not to react with anger but with a positive, peaceful thought.

What is not love is always fear. — G. Jampolsky. There are two basic emotions, all the things that feel like love and everything else. Anger, arrogance, pride and depression are based on fear. List your fears. Then work on letting them go.

I could see peace instead of this. You can change your perception. Look for the positive hidden in every negative. Choose peace.

Enlightenment is being able to go to your own home and feel comfortable. Happiness comes from the inside, not the outside. Remind yourself of what brings you joy and peace. Set a goal to bring more of these things into your life.

Very few things are truly important. You expend energy repeatedly for things that are not truly important to you or your community. Ask yourself over and over again, "What is truly important?"

Success is the quality of your journey, not a destination. Success is every moment of your life — the quality of your interaction with living things. Choose quality whenever you can.

SUCCESS

People we admire as having successful lives have similar traits.

- They have a purpose in life beyond themselves.
- They set goals and make plans.
- They envision their plans being successful.
- They don't get trapped in a comfortable "plateau" very long
- They solve problems, rather than blaming.
- They are optimistic, good-humored.
- They are concerned with quality, not just quantity.
- They understand they are in control.

All these traits are learned, not innate.

The definition of "success" and "quality of life" is yours alone.

Only you determine what brings to each day, joy, energy, passion and peace.

TODODAY

"Love all of life. Each year brings its own pleasures — and sings its own songs."

— *Flavia*

There is always the temptation to live in the past or the future. "Well, things will be better tomorrow." "I'll enjoy life more when the sun is out." "I never enjoy Mondays and I prefer June to March." "Things were better last year." "I'll be glad when this day, week, month or year is over."

It is possible with these thoughts to postpone your entire life waiting for the right moment.

We do it in work and relationships, too. "Oh, well, I'll put in a good day tomorrow." "I can be nice to her next time."

THIS IS THE MOMENT. Stop and put some joy, some quality, some awareness into it now; a smile, a squeeze, a sip, a smell, or just take a deep breath. Cherish YOUR life and hear the notes of each song. Up the scale or down, the music is always there.

THANK YOU

As I make plans for the New Year, I wonder how people who care about the world decide what to do.

I've been thinking about John Lennon.

It takes me a while sometimes to lay things to rest.

My son borrowed my car while I was away and left a Beatles tape in the tape player.

"Christ, you know it ain't easy. You know how hard it can be. The way things are going, they're going to crucify me."

Getting too far out in front, offering a different perception, taking chances, being transparent, looking for ways to honor your life and the life around you.

A moment of grace for all of you who try.

"Christ, you know it ain't easy..."

SLOW DOWN

I lost some good friends last year. A few friends died. I lost touch with some others who lived at too fast a pace and closed the year sick or depressed. It's time to slow down, not just to protect your health and relationships, but so you can see and feel more clearly.

There was a time when I felt I had to rush through life. There are so many good things to do. Nothing could stop me.

Ecstasy was a day when I got 25 errands accomplished, no red lights, the right parking space and no other customers in my way.

I've been learning this lesson for years, but this Christmas "the spirit" kept eluding me. I finally realized the Christmas spirit travels at 5 mph and I was traveling at 50. No time to hear music, smell pine boughs or feel anything.

There will always be many good, important things to do, but life is better measured by quality not quantity.

The new year is a time to decide again what is truly important. Take good care of yourself so next year you will not have lost friends or yourself.

I'll do it if you will.

BLISS

I was lucky enough recently to spend a few hours with Tom Robbins. He reminded me to check my sources of bliss.

Go back to when you were a child and think about what made you happiest. Tom remembered giving dramatic readings to an audience of trees. He's still telling his stories to the world and letting us share them.

I remembered the iridescent beauty of the dragonflies on Newman Lake outside Spokane and the bleeding-heart bush by our front door. I've planted more bleeding hearts in my own yard and am waiting for the dragonflies to visit my pond; they did last summer.

What are your sources of bliss? They are so simple, and yet many of us have lost touch. Close your eyes, take a deep breath and let the child within you smile.

PERSISTENCE

Improving our lives or environment always seems to cost more than we imagine. Making dreams come true requires hard work, risk, lots of doubt and times when we want to quit.

Remodeling a personality may in some ways compare to working on a house. You never really finish. There are surprises behind the walls and a feeling of disorientation when things are out of order, when patterns change. It's also easy for the neighbors to see what a mess you're in.

Sometimes all you are left with is your persistence. If you believe in yourself and want something enough, you keep working. On those cold, foggy mornings when you begin to question yourself or your latest project, remember why you're doing what you're doing. Remind yourself of your dreams; warm up your thoughts, and put one foot in front of the other.

SOLITUDE

"My passionate interest in social justice and social responsibility has always stood in curious contrast to a marked lack of desire for direct association with men and women. I am a horse for single harness, not cut out for tandem or team work. I have never belonged wholeheartedly to country or state, to my circle of friends, or even to my own family. These ties have always been accompanied by a vague aloofness, and the wish to withdraw into myself increases with the years.

"Such isolation is sometimes bitter, but I do not regret being cut off from the understanding and sympathy of other men. I lose something by it, to be sure, but I am compensated for it in being rendered independent of the customs, opinions, and prejudices of others, and am not tempted to rest my peace of mind upon such shifting foundations."

— Albert Einstein

VALENTINES

"There is no such thing as love, only acts of love."
— Picasso

Love is supposed to feel good. Yet many of us get caught thinking love hurts. Not being loved hurts. People will say, "I love you," while squeezing the knee of your best friend.

People will say, "I love you," and then not come home at night. "I love you," says the parent who is hitting the child. "This is for your own good," says the person handing us a slug. "I wouldn't do this if I didn't love you." Help. With all that love, we could end up depressed.

You can give love to yourself — I hope you will — only by acts of love and kindness. You can love others the same way.

Let us join together this Valentine's Day and sidestep the talk, the promises, the illusion of love and go all out for the real thing, the acts of love.

Love is something you do.

In the midst of winter I finally learned that there was in me an invincible summer. — A. Camus

RESENTMENT

Some African tribes believe forgiveness is essential to life. When a person falls ill, the relatives search for someone who harbors ill will. They assume a member of the family or tribe is holding onto resentments and causing the sickness. The patient will die if they will not forgive.

The reverse is also true when we hold resentment inside. When we cannot forgive, we deny ourselves health and our future because we remain stuck in the past.

There are those who say we must never forget history or personal attacks because we will not remember to protect ourselves in the future. Pain is an incredible teacher; we can learn and then let it go.

Forgive whenever you can. Work at it. Let go of guilt and resentment as tools of negotiation.

Your health, your survival and your peace of mind depend on your willingness to commit to tomorrow.

REST

It's time to relax. Put down all those lists, slow down your heartbeat, light a fire. Let the quiet before spring soothe the productive beast within you.

Take the whole day to relax and review your feelings, values and priorities. It doesn't mean you'll get behind. You'll get to see ahead.

Draw some sustenance into yourself before spring — deep breaths, solitude and peace.

You are much more than the sum of what you produce.

"THE CALL"

Throughout your life, there is a voice only you can hear. A voice mythologists label "the call." A call to the value of your own life. The choice of risk and individual bliss over the known and secure.

You may choose not to hear your spirit. You may prefer to build a life within the compound, to avoid the risk. It is possible to find happiness within a familiar box, a life of comfort and control.

Or, you may choose to be open to new experiences, to leave the limits of your conditioning, to hear "the call." Then you must act.

If you never hear it perhaps nothing is lost. If you hear it and ignore it, your life is lost.

REALITY

You can see this illustration at least two ways. One way offers conflict, one does not. We can choose to see the world in more than one way.

Reality is a matter of perspective.

There are many ways to victimize people, and one of the most insidious is to try to persuade them they are victims, that they have no choice.

If you think like a victim, you are a victim.

To change history, we need only to change ourselves. To change ourselves, we need only to change our minds. (Tom Robbins, Robert Anton Wilson)

SPRING

"All we do our whole lives is go from one little piece of holy ground to another."

— *J.D. Salinger*

I feel anticipation everywhere. It's time to wander in the garden and breathe in all the new energy of spring. I'm always amazed at what lies just underneath the surface of our world.

It's time to shrug off the grayness. Time to swell inside like the buds on the flowering plum. Time to feel the peace within, the balance around us.

Time to stop for the moments of pleasure and know they are for you.

WHO?

- *It's not my fault.*
- *There's just too much work.*
- *Why is she attacking me?*
- *He's got to change.*

There's nobody out there. There are only our perceptions of other people.

"It's not my fault" means I feel guilty for something and I resent it.

"Too much work" means I don't want to admit that I am making the choices.

Attacks from others always start from within. We attack ourselves, we bruise our self-esteem. Then we're convinced someone else is hurting us.

"He's got to change" because I refuse to.

There's nobody out there. Only you, alone with your choices and your perceptions.

HOT BUTTONS

Knee-jerk! Red herring! Flags waved in front of bulls! How often do you respond in a flash, without a thought?

I'm often a lightning rod for instant, intense reactions, so I've been mulling over what scares us, what creates that angry response.

Join me: What would you put on your list?

• Religion: Faith is usually bought in a tight box so we're afraid examination will destroy it all.

• Sex: Nothing scares us more than true intimacy and the resulting vulnerability.

• Patriotism: Our territorial instinct, our need to be safe, to be on the right side.

• Guns: Confusion about safety and aggression.

• Smoking: This is my air too!

• Pornography: Give them an inch, they'll take a mile.

Remember long hair, feminists, cults, rock 'n' roll, Vietnam?

Within each of us there are floating mines waiting to explode at the slightest touch. Find out what yours are, examine your fears, work out a resolution. Then the rest of us won't have to stay out of firing range.

TIME

"Love brings much more happiness than efficiency."

— *Ken Keyes Jr.*
"Handbook to Higher Consciousness"

High tech and multiple options surround us: communication at ever increasing speed and complexity. As our world changes faster, we move and think faster. Help! There is more to life than increasing its speed.

Happiness lies not in our interaction with inanimate objects but in our deep connection with life (people, animals, plants), especially your own.

Pleasure is all around if you can see, hear, smell and feel it. The lament "there's not enough time" is a signal to slow down and make contact. There is always just the right amount of time.

You can speed up your life if you want to, that's easy. Winding down is what's hard. Let go of the surface maintenance, dig a little deeper, take time to love.

SPACESHIP

This is a test! Turn your frequency to your best self and prepare for the future.

A spaceship is going to land in your front yard. Hummmmm, lights flashing, whirr, thunk! A door opens in the ship and a ramp descends to your feet. A bright light appears in the doorway and an unidentified arm beckons you up the ramp.

Are you going?

Are you going to wait and see what happens to your neighbor when he walks up before you decide?

Are you going to call the national guard?

End of test — did you pass?

What would a group of third graders have done? Up the ramp, fast — wow!

What's the difference between you and a third grader?

Experience? How much experience have you had with spaceships?

Perception?

You think any alien is after your stuff or your body — they think it's E.T.

Stephen Speilberg has given an entire generation of American children back the universe.

They're not afraid and we still are.

We see alien, they see friend.

It's time to open yourself to the world and the universe so you'll be ready when the invitation comes.

An invitation to be part of tomorrow.

ZEN

Two monks are walking along the road, and they come to a river. On the bank of the river is a beautiful young woman who is afraid to cross the river by herself. One of the monks gallantly steps forth and offers her a ride on his shoulders. Upon reaching the other side, she thanks the monk and they go their separate ways.

About one-hundred steps down the road, the second monk says to the first, "How could you do that? You are a monk, a renunciate. You should not be carrying beautiful women around on your shoulders."

To which the first monk replied, "Oh, are you still carrying her? I let her down when we reached the shore."

— a traditional Zen story

What are you still carrying around? Who are you carrying it for?

Like yourself now. Be ten years ahead of your friends.

ANOTHER CHANCE

The crocuses are up, the primroses are out and spring fever isn't far behind.

It's a great time of year because everything starts growing. Everything gets a second chance to bloom.

You do, too.

- Plant something to prove your optimism.

- Bring some branches in so the buds open early.

- Clean something, so it's fresh.

- Take a spring walk.

- Say "hello" to a neighbor; hibernation's over.

- Wake up earlier, with the light.

- Buy a bright spring sweatshirt.

This is it: time to stretch your body and mind, develop a few new shoots and check your buds.

CONTROL

Frustration, irritation, impatience, anger — the desire for control. We learn as children a terror of being at the mercy of events, situations and circumstances we cannot control.

Children of alcoholics and abusers have it burned into their soul.

The unpredictable grab or slap. The broken glass that becomes a hurricane.

You want it to be different for you. But no matter how you try, how thoughtful you are, you cannot control the spouse, kids, dogs, friends. You seeth with fear and frustration. One snip of the taut wire and it will all come apart and you'll be a child again — caught.

You dream of a place for everything and everything in it's place.

The fundamental mistake we make is the belief that we have a responsibility to bring order into life and everyone has a different sense of what that order should be. We assume because of our chaos that order is not natural; that disorder will occur if we do not impose on it. Slowly we realize that no amount of imposed order brings the control we hunger for.

Let go a little, just one corner or drawer, relax, stop trying to impose your order on the world. Give up the illusion that it's essential for your safety.

Shift a little each day away from your fear of chaos and towards acceptance of the natural harmony around you.

PATCHES

"The most beautiful people I have known are those who have known defeat, known suffering, known struggle, known loss, and have found their way out of the depths. These people have an appreciation, a sensitivity, and an understanding of life that fills them with compassion, gentleness, and a deep loving concern.

Beautiful people do not just happen."

— Historian Roy Nichols

Pain is a great teacher, but most of us would rather learn some other way. We think that happiness comes from a perfect childhood and avoiding mistakes. We don't like that patched-up feeling that comes with each survival. We would like to be seamless, no patches, no pits. Cherish your hard-won depth and understanding. Some pain is required for the journey. The gifts you seek are often disguised as problems.

Patches bring strength whether on our knees or in our hearts.

OPTIMISM

I often write about optimism. It is part of the change happening in our culture. It is an essential characteristic for peace. For too long we confused pessimism with intelligence. Pessimism is inherited from pessimistic adults; it is a form of depression that sees a negative past and no future.

Check your outlook.

You make the choice: You can be a serious — "I must be intelligent" — intense, miserable pessimist who's probably depressed.

You can be a lighthearted, philosophical optimist who may be perceived as less aware and intelligent but who is happy and at peace. Who has more to offer? Who may be more aware?

There is no way to feel fully alive unless you are willing to start your day with at least one optimistic option.

BEING

There is a subtle shift going on in our culture. We are changing from the "having" to the "being" mode.

The 1960's were a time of breaking loose because of the safety of our material foundation.

The 1970's were a time of introspection; we turned inward to check our values and ourselves.

The 1980's are a time to move toward being. It's time to overcome the myth of separation and material satisfaction.

Edward Lindeman, in his book "Thinking in the Future Tense," reminds us that material goods are basic to human existence, but they are not the source of joy or richness.

Joy is found in creativity, personal relationships, quality, peace, culture, the human spirit and connection with living things.

Check your sources of joy.

JUSTICE

It's hard to forgive when you feel you are under attack. The desire for justice can easily shift to a desire for revenge.

When you're in a situation that feels like an attack, try to understand why.

What pain is the other person acting out? Try to spend a moment seeing from their perspective.

Anger is always fear. Can you let go of your fear?

Can you accommodate their need, or is it endless?

Can you let go even if they cannot?

You can choose to forgive while protecting yourself. You can choose peace while facing conflict. You can offer love when facing anger. Or you can wait for justice as long as you remember:

Justice is much harder to find than peace.

FUTURES

Perhaps because it's spring, or maybe it's the influence of all the books and articles on the future — but the future is often on my mind.

Decide on your preferred future. Imagine it. Design it. Then work backward toward the present.

Check your visions: What do you want to happen?

Scout the terrain: What's already happening?

Imagine other possibilities: Invent your own hopes.

Make a commitment: Give power to the direction in which you decide to move.

What you imagine of the future determines what it will be. Quick! It starts now.

SIMPLE

It's camping season, the annual return to the woods.

The best style is as simple as possible: bread cooked in the coals, fish caught from the stream.

It's as if we need a reminder of the basics of life.

Camping gives us pleasure because of the profound simplicity of living without technology — the pleasure of concentrating on direct life-related work. No multiple-option tension here. Just the single options of catching and cooking, slow conversation, marveling at caterpillars and tree sap, sleeping at dusk, waking at dawn.

Simple, peaceful, a respite in a world addicted to speed and complexity.

Your body tingles when you remember the woods are always waiting — ready to restore your perspective by reminding you of what you really need to be happy: clean air, quiet, the natural environment and a rainbow you caught yourself.

SABBATICAL

It's time for you to take a sabbatical.

There are many theories about our need for a change of pace and environment: a respite, a chance to think, a challenge.

Sometimes we wait for illness or burnout to force us to take a breath, but it's easier to just choose to slow down, look a little deeper, take a personal Chautauqua.

The ingredients are basic: solitude, time, a physical or intellectual challenge, nature and a step outside the limits of our own culture.

The first sabbatical I took was to Grenada when it was an unknown, sleepy island. I stayed six weeks and replenished my body and soul. I was suffering then from too much growth too fast.

Now it's the opposite. I've been too busy to stretch in some of the ways I feel I need. This time I'm going to try mountains to pull me up and onward to the next turn in the path.

I've been in love with Mount Rainier for years. Now I'm going to Nepal to tromp around the base of Everest and Annapurna.

It's time for you to put more passion into your life. Join me, plan your own sabbatical now and then travel with me to the mountains.

LET'S TALK

People keep calling us to our best selves.

They want us to take care of our bodies and our minds. They remind us that we are mortal, and we still think in terms of forever.

Then the elbow creaks and the wrinkles multiply.

IT IS TIME TO HOLD A MEETING.

Sit down and hold a meeting with your body: Imagine 6,000 cells, each with human features and wearing a bright sweatshirt. Now explain to the liver cells why you are drinking things that make them sick. They want to know why they have to wear brown sweatshirts when they prefer red.

Talk to the cells in your lungs and explain why they cannot get their shirts clean. Explain to the stomach guys why they need ladders to avoid the fat that's floating around them.

Try to convince the muscle and tendon team that they should jump whenever you ring the bell, even if it's only once a month. They refuse to even dress.

Last but not least, after checking in with all your other cell friends, what about the sex cells? They are promised romance and they are getting either no action at all or no time to prepare their act.

True, this will be a long and difficult meeting, but they have been waiting a long time for you to show interest.

Negotiate, or prepare for a strike.

VISION

Marilyn Ferguson is working on another book. She is calling it "The Visionary Factor." The question: "Why are some people in the right place at the right time?"

Actually, all of us are, but we get educated out of our own vision. We disconnect our self-knowledge and connect with that of others. We lose touch with our sources of joy and imitate those of others.

As Marilyn puts it, the goal for all of us in the future is: "Not to get everything you want but to want everything you get."

CREDIT

Getting attention is an essential survival mechanism for a baby. If adults don't notice the baby crying it could starve. Getting attention also is essential for small children.

Many of us cannot shift from that small-child desire to be noticed and given credit to the adult system of internal credit.

Test yourself; can you share credit? Try giving credit to someone else that you might have kept for yourself.

How do you feel when no one notices your contribution?

Start measuring yourself by your personal value system.

You can get a lot more done if you don't care who gets the credit.

MALENESS

Women have asked, "When will men find themselves as women have?" Robert Bly has answered *"Men are finding that their strength lies not only in their newly acquired female sensitivities but in their deep masculine self."*

In their desire not to abuse the physical power of their maleness, some men have hesitated to show it. They have lost touch with their own depth and strength.

Don't confuse kindness with weakness. Don't confuse your energy force with violence. Stay in contact with your heart.

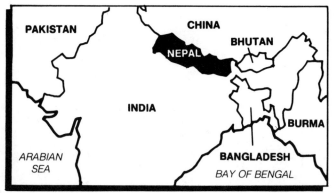

Map of Nepal

MOUNTAINS

I'm on another journey, struggling up some mountain in Nepal. My hikes are often the same. The journey toward the heart, the God within us.

Journey with me a little way up the mountain. Close your eyes, breathe the cool air, feel the solitude, step into another part of the spiritual world with me.

I'll do the puffing up the hill, and you can do the sharing of the spiritual load.

Every page while I climb, take a step yourself on your own spiritual journey. The journey toward the heart is always a journey home.

NEPAL JOURNEY I

It was difficult to sleep last night. Why wasn't I satisfied with something simple like going to Maui to lie in the sun? Why a trip to Katmandu and beyond?

I'm about to embark on a five-week journey, three of them hiking about 110 miles through the mountains in Nepal.

As I'm bouncing around in my head I remember a friend telling me to measure the moments of life I had left. She calls it "learning to be mortal." Make sure you know what you want because there is only so much time. Life is precious. I am proud — if scared — to be an adventurer.

Packing, savoring the moments of anticipation, squeezing my new down vest, running my fingers through hair cut short for the trek and choosing books worth carrying in my backpack. Peter Matthieson's *The Snow Leopard, Zen and the Art of Motorcycle Maintenance* by Robert Pirsig and *Letters Between Mothers and Daughters* edited by Karen Payne.

It's time to go, warming to my husband's support of my last minute jitters, his openness to my travels. Enjoying the company of my son, David, as he drives me around on last minute errands. Then at the airport he gives me a wonderful hug! We're not self-conscious anymore now that my head barely reaches his chin.

Ecstasy, I'm on the plane and there is an empty row so I can stretch out for the long flight. Flying makes me feel like a bird in a nest waiting to be fed. It's cozy but I wish I could fly myself.

Looking around the plane I'm reminded how different the world looks outside Seattle. Passengers on Seattle-Bangkok-Katmandu flight represent all colors, clothing styles and ethnicity: business men from Hong Kong, tourists from New Delhi, adventurers from everywhere. Somehow I'm one of them.

* * *

SOMETHING MORE

"I am sure there is something more."

"If only I could meet the right man or woman."

There is something more. The feeling of belonging to a family, a love for your brothers and sisters that has nothing to do with couples.

The family is the human one. The love is shown through concern for the future and for those who are at risk. That love is at least as valid and rewarding as the love we try to give to just one person.

We get lost in loneliness looking for a single mate when there is a whole world waiting. The impulse to mate is powerful, but there is a shift taking place on our planet, a shift toward connecting with the spirit in others, a shift away from couples in little boxes.

"There is no enterprise which is started with such tremendous hopes and expectations and which fails so regularly as romantic love."
— *Erich Fromm*

There is no love that rewards with more consistency and provides lifelong passion as the love one has for the world.

PY

I spent an afternoon with Py Bateman last week. She gave me a powerful gift: the belief that I could fight for my life if I had to and the determination to do it.

Py is the director of Alternatives to Fear. She has spent 14 years teaching women to protect themselves from sexual violence. Py has always believed intensely in what she was doing even when her sisters sometimes doubted.

A few weeks ago, Py was brutally attacked outside her home on a sunny afternoon. She was cut up, beaten and ended up in critical condition, but she fought off her attacker. Py is petite; she cut her hands deeply pulling the knife away from her throat. She told me that throughout the long attack, they fought all over her house; she was determined to hold on, to keep control of herself. She cannot remember when it stopped and she lapsed into unconsciousness.

We sat across a table, Py with her hospital haircut, scars from brain surgery, scars around her eyes from the knife, scars on her hands. She told me that she was planning to work even harder to teach women to conquer their fear. She knew it might save their lives.

Sitting with Py I felt afraid. I felt a new determination. I felt loved.

MORTALITY

I am learning to be mortal.

For such a long time I felt age or death could not touch me. Yet, I've been thinking about my older friends. We're putting a bathroom on our first floor so they can visit without the indignity of being carried upstairs.

We still design our homes and lives as if we will live forever. Learning to be mortal requires you to take much better care of yourself and your friends.

Time then becomes an ally to cherish and enjoy, not an enemy always speeding ahead.

Keep your connections with the older generations strong. They will share the wisdom and humor of time, remind you of your own mortality and encourage you to live deeply and well.

OLYMPICS

The Olympics are wonderful. For a moment in time, fixed on the glowing faces of athletes and artists, anything seems possible.

We believe again in hard work, courage and reward. We believe again that nations have more in common than in conflict.

Olympic athletes have learned that both body and mind must work together. They have learned to visualize their goal.

The values are clear, the imperfections tolerable. The ethic survives: Winning is still not as important as how you play the game.

How about an Olympics of the heart? A competition for clarity, centeredness and peace?

Anyone ready to carry the torch to thread families, states and nations together? Hard work, courage and the ability to see the goal is all it takes. Start with your own team. Stretch the muscles of your mind and heart.

We'll cheer you on. But only you will know if you've got the gold.

INTIMACY

The desire for intimacy with another human being seems as strong as life itself: It's the desire to escape the isolation, the aloneness of our human uniqueness. We confuse this desire so often with sex that we no longer can understand what we want.

"Sex can be and often is specialized and standardized. Love is always unique, one of a kind.

"Sex strives for reliability and predictability. Love is eternally surprising."

— George Leonard

Intimacy requires commitment on a deeply personal level; an affirmation of life, a commitment to know ourselves and to know another. The rewards are great: tenderness, exaltation, transformation. Leonard calls such commitment "high monogamy." It is the opposite of sex as exercise.

We all seek ecstacy, but fear leads us to sabotage our own joy — the joy in our ability to love, to create, to feel deeply.

TRUST

I want to help create more trust.

We don't trust each other enough. We are afraid of steps toward common values. We think we will be controlled, not enhanced, if we agree on certain things together.

It took us a long time to trust our society enough to invade individual freedom and begin to put pressure on drunken drivers. Now we are beginning to trust that we won't use a breathalyzer to hurt, but to prevent hurt.

It's taking us a long time to understand that we won't voraciously invade family privacy if we try to help abused children.

We're just beginning to feel we might stop molesters by taking away their access to children and that it does not represent a loss of freedom but a gain for the freedom of children.

We're stuck when it comes to violent and child pornography. Librarians say if we remove one magazine, we will want to remove them all. Why do we have so little faith in ourselves? Why is it considered impossible to balance freedom with limits on displays of violence toward women and children?

I trust myself, I trust you, I trust our basic values and our deliberative process. It's time to take care of each other, it's safe to take care of each other, it's possible to take care of each other.

DREAMS

There are all sorts of dreams floating by.

Dreams are an essential part of our creativity, as long as we make them a real part of our life.

If you dream of a better job, writing the great American novel, being svelte or building a greenhouse, the question is: What step however small, have you taken toward that vision?

If you dream of a genie who pops out of the bottle and cleans the whole house, why not clean out just one drawer yourself?

Lottery dreams are of security, not having to work, new cars, trips around the world, gifts to those you love. What can YOU do while you wait, or in the off-chance that you don't win?

Pipe dreams are when you don't trust your own dreams and use alcohol or some other drug to squelch or alter your visions. Skip those detours.

Life is filled with dreams and possibilities. Spend your dream time traveling as far as you can; cherish your imagination. Then cherish your reality by taking a small step toward making your dreams come true.

LET GO

It's hard to let go. We hold on to investments, habits, relationships and defenses long after our awareness that they are hurting us.

We notice the problem, like a light going on, then ignore it. If we ignore what we know, we think we won't lose all we thought we had.

Investment in the past usually increases our losses, but we still choose the dull ache over the brief confrontation with grief.

It's like keeping yourself on simmer for a lifetime instead of high for a second.

Learn to cut your losses, not hide them. Time to let go and leap forward.

"We shall not cease from exploration and the end of all our exploring will be to arrive where we started and know the place for the first time. — T.S. Eliot

NEPAL JOURNEY II

Flying from Bangkok to Nepal. Waiting with all the other pilgrims for that first view of the Himalayas, "the top of the world." The plane shudders as everyone tries to lean out the windows on the right side.

As the mountains come into view they seem so much more than mountains to those of us raised with a view of Mt. Rainier. Jagged, immense, many Everests, not just one. Mt. Everest hardly is noticed amid so many rough giants. I'm out of words, slipping into a philosophical trance thinking of all the spires humans create to reach heaven and as usual natural architecture is light years ahead.

The view slips away as we descend through the clouds and drop to views of steeply terraced hillsides, level upon intricate level stacked up on a hillside until they disappear into the clouds and give way to the Himalayas.

I plan to spend three days seeing Katmandu, Nepal's capital city; go by bus for four days to the jungle of the Royal Chitwan National Park near the India border, then trekking in the Annapurna peaks of the Himalayas.

Katmandu is one grand bazaar of noise and color and smell. Incense, bells, wandering sacred cows, dogs, ducks, chickens and cars in the same streets. Music and garbage everywhere. Spices, textiles, art, all mixed with bicycle parts and American sweatshirts.

I am staying at a tiny hotel run by an elegant Hindu woman. The Nepalese I have met are gentle, helpful, willing to please although they have seen many Western visitors. One of the streets has been renamed Freak Street in our honor. Most Nepalese speak a little English.

The food is good — rice and oatmeal porridge. Lots of hot curry and cookies I call "coconut crunchies." I am reveling in the chance to share other worlds. It amazes me to find the same flowers wherever I travel. The Katmandu market is full of marigolds. People everywhere, no matter how poor, always grow a plant or two in a pot on the roof or in front of the door, even the smallest hut.

There are wonderful tiny oranges. I'm glad they're included in the "peel it, boil it, or forget it" advice to travellers.

* * *

UPDATE

When did you last update your perception of your past?

Sometimes we decide the quality of our childhood at 21 and hold on to it as if it were written in stone.

Then we grow, maybe raise our own children, get to know our family in a new way, and re-evaluate.

Negatives become positives. Positives may become negatives. Our perception changes.

Update, talk to your relatives, gather their view of the past. Try to understand what their motivations and problems were.

A critical mother may have been buckling under her own pain. A tough father may have been terrified for your safety. Love doesn't always end up feeling like love. We all mix up our motivations and make mistakes.

Update, understand, accept, forgive, let go and choose your future.

FILTERS

We've heard that we are what we think, that we get to choose how we see our world.

We know that people often live up or down to our expectations.

Perception is a filter that turns our view toward darkness or light. It can be an open view that sees good things happening or a closed view that only sees negative.

So much power.

The power to be open or closed to goodness.

MEDITATION

Meditation is humanity's oldest spiritual discipline. We all know the peace that comes from looking at a still pool, a sunrise or deep into a flower, or from experiencing the sounds of silence. A moment of pure joy and oneness.

It is the "satori" of Zen, the "samadhi" of the yoga and is a path to St. Paul's "the peace that passeth understanding."

Meditation is available to you in many forms: prayer, stargazing, deep-breathing, chanting, trance or just slowing down.

It reduces tension, enhances your awareness of life, increases joy and adds to self-discipline and self-knowledge.

Some call meditation an altered state of consciousness, but it is only the peace waiting beneath the surface of your busyness.

A moment of joy, always available as a gift for you, by you, to you and to all of us.

Stop now to sense the rhythm within. Take a deep breath, connect for a moment with all life. The power, the energy, the joy of the whole.

A minute a day for peace.

THE SEARCH

"The great and venerable Sufi sage, Mullah Nasrudin, once raced through Baghdad on his donkey, galloping as fast as the poor beast could travel. Everybody got excited and people rushed into the streets to find out why the philosopher was in such a great hurry.

" 'What are you looking for, Mullah?' somebody shouted.

" 'I'm looking for my donkey!' Nasrudin answered.

We look for the secret... in all directions... and all the time it is carrying us about."
Robert Anton Wilson (in "The Cosmic Trigger")

All you need lies within.

FAMILY

Next time you find yourself lamenting that your family wasn't perfect, remember that you have three families.

First there is the family you are born into, then the family you may join to survive the transition from home to your own home, and last there is the family you build yourself.

The most important of these families is the one you build yourself. It may include people from the other two, but you get to decide. Think about whom you want in your family. What kind of qualities are you looking for? Then gradually add those people to you life. Work on improving relationships with your first two families.

Build a home and family that is safe and loving for you.

Your family is your choice.

VALUES

There is a concern in the land about values. What is happening to people's morals? How can I teach my children values?

There is agreement among some who study human behavior that the development of values can be set up as a sequence of levels, ranked from lowest to highest:

- Fear of punishment.
- Exchange (You give to me, I'll give to you)
- Expectations (Meet my expectations, get a reward.)
- Law and order (Civilization requires control.)
- Principles (I will act according to my beliefs even if I do not personally gain.)
- Fairness (the Golden Rule.)
- Quality of life for everyone, everywhere.

Check your decisions. On what levels do you make your choices? Very few of us get close even to the level where we act on principles, but we keep trying.

Success is determined by our interaction with living things, not by our collection of inanimate objects. It is the quality of the journey that ultimately brings satisfaction.

PERSPECTIVE

If you wait long enough, things are supposed to look better. It's called perspective, the magic of knowing what matters. The problem is how to get it when you need it.

The next time something happens to get you down, try the "family-album trick."

Imagine yourself 20 years from now sitting in front of the fire reminiscing. Things that were once heartbreakers seem silly or funny. Problems you never thought you could solve worked out. Grief gradually added depth and quality to your life.

Perspective — what made you cry at 6 is unimportant at 26. Add 20 years to your evaluation of problems and chuckle.

Remind yourself of what is truly important.

Keep the magic in your life.

I am never upset for the reason I think.

NEPAL JOURNEY III

Katmandu is still ringing in my ears, but it's time to board a bus to Southern Nepal and the National Wildlife Refuge. Nepalese roads are amazingly steep. Just imagine a multiplication of the old Lewiston grade in Idaho, add incredible steep cliffs and no shoulders and then close your eyes.

There are very few roads in Southern Nepal and none in the north because of the mountains. Many people still walk everywhere and I pass many travellers trudging up and down the hills.

People who ride do so in gaudily decorated 1940's square trucks. Big trucks, like army transport with people and goods stuffed in the back.

The farms we pass are the same terraces I glimpsed from the plane. Very much like China, a patch work quilt but with many more levels. Lots of water buffalos and no evidence of mechanization except the occasional car on the road.

Many areas of Nepal are referred to by the euphemism "food deficit area" to indicate that people are barely subsisting. But Southern Nepal looks more productive and less close to the line. Produce is everywhere, melons even grow on people's roofs.

Nepal is one of the most beautiful places I have ever been. Poinsettas seem as big as houses and orchids hang out of the trees. At the road end I am picked up by a land rover to ford the river, enter the park and the jungle.

My home now is a small cabin on one side of a broad river, and in the dusk I can see the jungle across the river and hear the elephants trumpeting.

My internal time clock is dizzy so I awaken just before dawn and creep out to sit by the Dungre River that flows by the camp. Fog is slowly rising, herons are fishing and a crew of elephants are already at work with the "manhout" in charge, gathering food for the elephant camp. The elephants gather huge tree branches to forage on.

At breakfast I meet Maria, attracted to her small table by the energy she throws around the room. She is 71, a Hungarian gymnastics teacher who has just climbed all the way to the Everest base camp near the border with China. Full of the adventure, she describes the beauty of the mountains and the trekker who died on the trail she was on. Two or three of every thousand trekkers die because of the altitude and lack of transportation or medical care she notes. "Not to worry" she then says to me.

I'm a little uncomfortable at a jungle camp designated for tourists but the guides are naturalists or seem to be well informed, the money is used to preserve the refuge.

The day includes a ride in the jungle behind the ears of an elephant. It's like bareback riding except bigger. The fog is still with us as my elephant crunches into the jungle. I'm thinking "lions and tigers and bears" but in fact we see deer, rhinoceroses and peacocks.

Another dawn; steam is rising from the jungle as penny-sized drops of dew plummet down on me from the trees. I'm thinking about the New Year. Last night talking with Australians, Nepalese and Indians thinking: "What are you going to give to the world next year? How will you keep your give and take in balance?"

I am beginning to slip into Nepalese time, to relax. There is no sense of Armageddon here. Time will continue to unfold and re-cycle.

It is time to leave the jungle and head to the mountains. I cannot wait to launch myself into the sky like a paper airplane. The bus leaves me in Pokhara, a jump-off city for trekkers. Looming high above the town is the first Himalayan peak I see from land, Machhapuchare, the "Fishtail", 22,940 feet. It is breathtaking, pink and utterly magnificent at dusk.

Trudging to my lodging through the dusty, dirty, anything but picturesque town, I am startled when I find I must cross a small lake on a tiny raft to reach my hotel, the Fishtail Lodge.

*   *   *

CONTRACTS

Was she really that jealous?

Once upon a time she had been. Yes, when they had first fallen in love. But that was years ago. Now what she felt as jealousy was really only habit.

To put it another way, every love relationship is based on unwritten conventions rashly agreed upon by the lovers during the first weeks of their love. On the one hand, they are living a sort of dream; on the other, without realizing it, they are drawing up the fine print of their contracts like the most hard-nosed of lawyers. O lovers! Be wary during those perilous first days! If you serve the other party breakfast in bed, you will be obliged to continue same in perpetuity or face charges of animosity and treason!

In those first weeks it was decided betwen Karel and Marketa that Karel would be unfaithful and Marketa would submit, but that Marketa would have the privilege of being the better one in the couple and Karel would always feel guilty. No one knew better than Marketa how depressing it was to be better.

— "The Book of Laughter and Forgetting" by
Milan Kundera

SELF-ESTEEM

Everything you see, hear, feel and evaluate is filtered through your self-esteem.

Our personal filters are built on a four-fold foundation.

• Fate: where you are born, when you are born, whether you are disabled, your race, sex and ethnicity.

• Family: rich or poor, supportive or abusive, together or separated.

• Experience: how many brick walls you run into, pits you fall into, accidents.

• Perception: how you perceive your fate, family and experience.

The most important element in self-esteem is your perception. The same circumstances produce those who can love and be loved and those who cannot.

SPARK

An interviewer asked Robert Schuller, minister at Crystal Cathedral, how he would like to be remembered. He answered:

"As someone who respected people and encouraged them... In the presence of hope, faith is born. In the presence of faith, love becomes a possibility. In the presence of love, miracles happen. I would like to be remembered as somebody who inspired, who ignited a spark of hope where there was only discouragement. If I ignite a spark of hope, probably I have produced the possibility of faith, and then love becomes a possibility. Finally, in the presence of love, miracles happen."

How would you like to be remembered?

LOVE

The theme song from the "Mary Tyler Moore Show" was "Love Is All Around," yet often we cannot see it.

We imagine love as "the grand passion," the lifetime commitment, not as available everywhere.

Love is caring and support. It's available from friends, relatives, neighbors, clerks, strangers, colleagues and people who wave from passing tour buses. You just need to know the rules.

First Rule of Love:
Love is something you do.

All the other rules:
Believe in its presence, make it a priority, assume love will last, share interests, be affectionate, forgive easily, love yourself and share your dreams.

Remember, love is a "game of flex."

Take as many bending-over-backward steps as you can without losing your identity.

FLEXIBILITY

Check your flexibility. Make sure you haven't locked into place.

Every year, do you give every vegetable a second chance? Or did you make your decisions at 12? "Lima beans will never cross my lips."

Do you experiment with new colors? Or do you stick with whatever you decided on at 14? "Plain girls shouldn't wear bright colors."

Do you dream of having everything perfect, clean, orderly? "Why do I have to live with slobs?"

When did you last try a new route to work?

How many friends do you have who are different from you (race, religion, ethnicity)?

What new skill did you learn last month?

Check your tension level, shake your shoulders and your mind. Loosen up.

Let the energy of the universe flow through you.

VIEWPOINT

I just finished a future workshop.

I was jogged again into my commitment to try to make a difference. What most of us want, simplified, is peace of mind, peace in the world and a piece of the action. When we get stuck with a single perspective, the one we were raised with or have held onto from childhood experience, we think it is essential for survival.

All of us need a new viewing point, a way to see alternative strategies.

Morris Massey suggests we give ourselves a chance to rise above our limits and history to another point of view instead of locking into position out of fear and habit.

Relax — use humor, meditate, count to 10, pray, go for a walk or run.

Insulate — find your "hot buttons" and protect them so you can see clearly.

Scan — look at all the possibilities, include every strategy, path, solution, use your imagination.

Sympathize — imagine how other people see and feel things, spend a moment on their path with their history.

The truth includes all points of view.

We are all in this together.

NEPAL JOURNEY IV

I start this day with porridge and watch my first sunrise over the Himalayas. Oatmeal always reminds me of my mother and cold mornings in Spokane. I am a little apprehensive after meeting with Minma the Sherpa that I will travel with.

He speaks little English and wants to take a different trail, one I fear is too difficult for me. We compromised and the porridge bolsters my faith in this trip. It's like carrying mother in my stomach. She helped instill in me this sense of adventure so I'm glad she's in my thoughts.

Minma and I set off together. My backpack of about 30 pounds holds my water, clothing, flashlight, knife, instant coffee and cup, first-aid kit, a few small oranges and my new down vest. Minma's pack holds food, a small tent, sleeping bags and extra boots.

We walk through the bazaar, the Tibetan refugee camp, across a valley and to the end of the road where there are other trekking groups of about 25 with porters and guides. I prefer just me.

This is the point of commitment. There will be no more vehicles of any kind, the paths are narrow and steep. A group of small pack horses pass by with bells ringing carrying A.I.D. rice from Japan.

I climb and climb until I am counting steps, resting and counting another fifty. In four hours I climb 3,000 feet.

Multiple terraces as far as I can see. The path is so steep that it is made of rock steps with groves worn by centuries of hooves and bare feet. This is the main trade route through Nepal between India and Tibet and merchants and travellers have walked this path for three thousand years.

At the top of this pass we camp on a ledge that seems to overlook all of Nepal. The clouds part and I can reach out and almost touch the jagged peaks.

There's no way I can describe these mountains. They make beautiful Mt. Rainier look like a sedate seed pearl next to these immense, roughly cut diamonds.

At the ocean, the other extreme, I always feel like a grain of sand caught in a brief moment of endless time. The feeling is stronger here. These mountains have been here forever and they are untouched, unworn, as if they had risen out of the earth in a jagged thrust only moments ago. The Himalayas were formed when the continents of India and China crashed together. So much power in a landscape of such peace.

It will take 25 days to reach the Tibetan border on foot depending on weather and speed. Two months would take me through Tibet and into China. I am only going halfway but already I want to come back and go further.

Time to crawl into my sleeping bag, mind boggled, muscles complaining of disuse and misuse. Time to sleep under the stars, so big and so close they seem only a cold puff of breath away.

*　　*　　*

"THE KIDS"

Concerns are beginning to surface about the music, clothes and video of "the kids."

Their passion for extremes scares us. They push the limits in everything: different drugs, sexual image, sexual activity, anti-war protest.

They make their fears and confusions explicit. We prefer ours hidden, but the difference is not that great:

Once Mae West pushed the limit, now it's Madonna.

Once it was Noel Coward, now it's Boy George.

Once it was Liberace, now it's Prince.

Once it was Gene Vincent, now it's punk rockers.

It's the classic generation gap. Are you tempted to find foreboding in their creativity, their passion?

Our kids are just probing the same themes, the same confusions, the same realities we have for decades, playing with their fears and establishing their identity as a new wave.

I wouldn't want to be part of a culture that didn't grow and stretch with each generation.

They will find their center, somewhere in our shared culture. They always come home to the basic rhythm that beats within all of us.

ZIP

"If we are going to do anything as simple as tightening a screw or as sublime as making a spiritual breakthrough, an adequate supply of gumption is the first and most important tool."

— *Thomas Crutcher*

Do you have gumption? How much? How many of these terms apply to you?

spirited	courageous	bold
fearless	excited	funny
confident	audacious	zippy
adventurous	thrilled	humorous
chutzpah	pizazz	daring
panache	spontaneous	bodacious

What's your gumption level? Happiness requires action of the mind, heart and body. Take a chance; believe in yourself.

We always gain from risk, the full commitment to our power and energy.

Zip-a-dee-doo-dah, zip-a-dee-yay... my, oh my, what a wonderful day!

GRACE

"I want, in fact — to borrow from the language of the saints — to live 'in grace' as much of the time as possible. I am not using this term in a strictly theological sense. By grace, I mean an inner harmony, essentially spiritual, which can be translated into outward harmony. I am seeking perhaps what Socrates asked for in the prayer from 'Phaedrus' when he said, 'May the outward and inward man be at one.' I would like to achieve a state of inner spiritual grace from which I could function and give as I was meant to in the eye of God."

"Vague as this definition may be, I believe most people are aware of various periods in their lives when they seem to be 'in grace' and other periods when they feel 'out of grace' even though they may use different words to describe these states. In the first happy condition, one seems to carry all one's tasks before one lightly, as if borne along on a great tide; and in the opposite state one can hardly tie a shoestring."

— Anne Morrow Lindbergh, "Gift From the Sea"

Whenever I read thoughts on inner peace, I'm struck by the element of choice. We know when we feel centered. We can feel the energy and ecstasy that harmony gives us.

At any given moment, we choose our response. We can choose grace or conflict, positive or negative.

Always reach for the highest-level universe, the one you want to operate in, as much of the time as possible.

CHICKENS AND EAGLES

What you are depends on what you believe to be true about yourself. We see ourselves and our world as we want so see it.

You have the choice. You are free to accept who and what you really are.

Check your philosophy of life. Here are two of the many alternatives available to you:

Philosophy of the Chicken	**Philosophy of the Eagle**
We lack something.	We lack nothing, we have everything and are everything.
We need something outside ourselves to make us feel secure.	The source of security and happiness comes from within.
When you give something, you lose it.	When you give, you receive and are blessed many times over.
Seek and do not find.	Seek and you shall find.
We are a body.	We are Mind and Spirit.
We are sinners.	We are a Child of God.
We are separate beings.	We are One.
We are destroyed by death.	Life is eternal.
The motivation and glue that holds us together are fear, anger and guilt.	The motivation and glue that holds us together are love, freedom, peace and joy.

"From a Chicken to an Eagle," by
Jerry Fankhauser, M.S.W.

HAPPINESS

Happiness is a perception of our mind, not a reflection of our situation. On days when everything goes wrong — mistakes, accidents, rejections, noise — we can still be happy.

Hugh Prather describes a mental state, "the grounds for happiness," that passes gently and easily over the endless nonsense that carpets the day.

Be happy being yourself no matter what the day brings.

RISK

"Security is mostly a superstition. It does not exist in nature, nor do the children of men as a whole experience it. Avoiding danger is no safer in the long run than outright exposure. Life is either a daring adventure or nothing."

— Helen Keller

There is no way to grow and stretch without taking risks. If you want to feel more, be more and give more — it's time to take chances.

David Viscott divides risk into seven phases:

- Recognizing your need to risk
- Deciding to risk
- Initiating the risk
- The point of no return
- Completing the risk
- Adapting to the change
- Evaluating the results

Start now with baby steps. As you become more comfortable trusting yourself, you can shift to bigger ones.

Give yourself a chance.

CHOICE

We are all able to choose happiness but most of us prefer not to. We are stuck in a pattern of guilt and recrimination.

There are many examples of people who have chosen peace and joy in the midst of loss. It doesn't lessen the loss, it just gives what remains value.

Martin Luther King (Senior)	Gloria Vanderbilt
Helen Keller	Mother Teresa
Ted Kennedy Jr.	Jacque Cousteau
Jesus Christ	Sam Smith
Harriet Tubman	Betty Ford
Py Bateman	Max Clelland
Maya Angelou	Terry Fox
Patricia Neal	Anne Jillian
Dan Deardorff	John Merrick (Elephant Man)
Anne Morrow Lindbergh	Jill Kinmont
William Least Heat Moon	

Make up your own list of people you know. Then add your self to·it.

I am making the choices.

NEPAL JOURNEY V

The days become an enchanting series of highs and lows. Up thousands of steps and then descending the same number into small villages. The village of Birathanti is especially beautiful. It lies across a cable bridge, over a raging river and looks like a paradise painted by Gauguin: bright flowers and fabrics, doorways and windows painted in bright designs — all edged by waterfalls. Hot tea, Tibetan fry bread, and the chance to rest.

After several days my senses catch up with me and I force myself to bathe in one of the icy streams that carries water from the Annapurna snows. Yikes!

Tonight the stars are even more incredible, the sky is so clear and deep. Orion looks as it must have to herdsman long ago. Close enough to feel the warriors breath and count the jewels in his scabbard. Cephia, the queen, looks real as she lounges only inches above the mountain peaks.

I'm sleeping in a farmyard nearby the water buffalos. I've filled my water bottle with hot water and rolled it to the bottom of my sleeping bag, ecstasy.

The trail is so beautiful, valley upon valley, waterfalls more beautiful than any I have ever seen, as I climb hour upon hour straight up. It must have been obvious to everyone that you would have to go up and down on this path but it just dawns on me today. The first great breakthough "the Himalayas are up and down." It only seems profound if your body is involved. Nothing I read had prepared me for the steepness.

The subject of suffering comes to mind. There are, of course, two kinds of suffering, that which has a reward and that which doesn't. I've always tried to avoid the latter — time to pull out the chocolate bar I stashed in my pack in Seattle.

Minma was prepared to cook all the meals, but after several days we began eating most meals in what are called "tea" houses, thatched homes in small towns along the trail which cater to trekkers.

The food is heavy with grains (oatmeal and breads of all sorts), vegetables often covered with a mildly spiced curry sauce, lots of eggs and an occasional chicken. Some small apples and oranges were available, but never milk.

I compare notes and eat with trekkers from all over the world at these tea houses. But as we climb higher and farther, we meet fewer and fewer people on the trail.

Minma, about 30 and a farmer when he's not a guide, is like a shadow to me. He speaks a little English, but we never really chat.

At rest, after nine hours of climbing, I sit with the stars again. The words of the Don McClean song "Vincent" swirl around me. "Starry, starry night. This world was never made for one as beautiful as you." Van Gogh might have changed his perspective if he had seen these stars.

Sleep is easy to come by here. It is so quiet, a hen and her seven chicks settle in only an arms length away. Lentils and rice settle easily in my full stomach.

*   *   *

SATISFACTION

Happiness is a controversial emotion. Those that exude it can be irritating and we assume uninformed. If you really knew what was going on you'd be a little more thoughtful about being happy.

When I suggest happiness is a choice, a perspective, I usually get an aargh or two.

New research on happiness reports it's a cultural (i.e. national) attribute. Some nations are simply happier than others.

Happiness ranking (from "Studies in Subjective Well-Being" by Ronald Inglehart)

1. Ireland	9. France
2. Great Britain	10. Finland
3. Netherlands	11. Spain
4. Denmark	12. West Germany
5. United States	13. Japan
6. Belgium	14. Italy
7. Sweden	etc.
8. Norway	

Happiness depends on satisfaction and satisfaction doesn't always correlate with income, strife, religion or education. These surveys have remained consistent since the start of this research in 1974.

So, if culture (i.e. perspective) is the dominant factor in the happiness formula, it's time to either choose to be happy or move.

SEPTEMBER

September is one of my favorite times because it promises a new beginning just when I was thinking I would miss summer. While others go off to school, start on a journey of your own, a journey toward self-knowledge and intimacy.

"The more I am truly myself, the more I can truly be one with you. The more I am truly one with you, the more I can be truly myself... High Monogamy... requires that we look directly and unflinchingly at our every weakness... to the very heart of our intentionality."

— George Leonard

What do you know about your intentionality? Leonard says the examination takes vertiginous daring. That translates as "whirling or dizzying," and sounds wonderful. Join me in a personal class with you as the teacher, a vertiginous examination of our intentionality, or simpley the journey toward the heart.

WINNING

"We were a little tentative in the first half," Seahawks quarterback Dave Krieg said. *"I was throwing off my back foot. Sometimes when you want to do everything just right, you play it too close to the vest."*

Coach Chuck Knox delivered a halftime message, Krieg said, *"to go out and have fun, to let it go."*

Watch out for the serious this season. Remember to relax, chuckle, sing, appreciate the light side. Let it go, let it happen, let it in. That's how most of us win, and even if we don't, we know we won't lose.

CRITICISM

Criticism has lost power recently as a way to control others. Encouragement, according to parenting and management theories, works much better. But it's hard to change the patterns of a lifetime.

Much of our history was spent struggling. We weren't thinking about the quality of life, only the quantity — survival. Criticism was used to control and motivate children. We wanted them to be "tough enough" for a difficult world.

Our survival needs have changed. We've begun to evaluate quality, to talk about love, personal awareness, relationships, communication and family strength. Instead of a negative power over others, we talk of empowering others.

Criticism has become dysfunctional. It builds resentment, fear and undermines confidence. We now have a world where inner strength is essential to success.

Love, support, encouragement help build values important to the quality of our future, values that will reduce personal violence, not increase it.

Let go of the negative. Survival now is much more likely to depend on the positive.

WELL-BEING

"Like the dance of brilliant reflection on a clear pond, well-being is a shimmer that accumulates from many important life choices made over the years by a mind that is not often muddied by pretense or ignorance, and a heart that is open enough to sense people in their depths and to intuit the meaning of most situations."
— *"Pathfinders" by Gail Sheehy*

FORGIVE

You did the best you could with who you were and what you knew at the time. As soon as you learned something better, you did that.

So why can't you forgive yourself and others for past mistakes?

For some people, punishment is not enough, atonement insufficient, retribution never satisfying. They wallow in guilt. They refuse to forgive themselves or others. They lose the future because they are trapped in the past.

Search out the painful mistakes in your past and prepare a certificate of forgiveness, complete with a gold seal for each one.

Maybe you'll give one to an adult child:

"I did the best I could... I wasn't a perfect parent... Here's a blanket apology... Let's end the criticism."

Give one to your spouse to end some past recrimination.

Give one to yourself: "I'm not perfect... I made a mistake..."

Create your certificates, forgive yourself. Then, sit down, relax, breathe deeply.

Let go of the guilt, let go of the past, breathe in the present and stay open to your future.

WOODENHEADEDNESS

Folly, as defined by historian Barbara Tuchman, is the pursuit of a policy contrary to your self-interest. Folly occurs when we seek power, ignore evidence, lack flexibility and are unable to reverse. She calls it **"woodenheadedness."**

"It's a lot easier to get your way if you have more than one way."

— Anonymous

There is no such thing as love, only acts of love. — Picasso

NEPAL JOURNEY VI

Today another hard climb, 6,000 feet. We reach the village where we will camp and I climb another 1,000 feet to the top of Pun Hill 10,200 feet with a 360 degree view of the mountains. Peak after peak surrounding me. The guide tells me that every year the King of Nepal comes here by helicopter to survey his land. It is freezing on this hill top and there is ice on the puddles when I climb down and into my sleeping bag. Many nights we sleep under the stars. When it's cold or rainy, we use the tent or sleep in closet-size rooms in people's houses opened to trekkers...

The Nepalese have a better way of keeping warm. They are dancing in the hut next door. Stamping their feet, beating drums, chanting, laughing, late into the night. I fall asleep to their drums...

The trail today winds down into a valley that reminds me of the rain forests of the Olympic Peninsula. It feels like a jungle, moss hanging from trees, ferns everywhere. I keep passing water buffalo. They use neither harness nor nose ring here. Their buffalo look so fierce but are very gentle. All of the many animals I have encountered on this trek are gentle. Gentle people, gentle animals. I have yet to see or hear a squabble, a raised voice, a whip or stick being used. The animals are everywhere, as we pass through villages, on the path, in the house all with young nearby. Chickens, ducks, pigs, dogs, small horses, burros and water buffalo. Along all the paths I travel I am greeted, even by small children, with hands together as in prayer, head gently bowed, and the word "Namaste." The greeting translates as "I salute the Spirit within you..."

The forest I am walking through today is full of rhododendrons, orange trees and orchids, an unexpected combination.

My feet are beginning to drag when another trekker passing tells me there is a hot spring outside of the next town, Tatopani. Just one hill and a cable bridge away. The dust of a week disappears in a Nepalese hot tub.

I feel at home now. My muscles are shaping up, I can walk ten miles a day even if it is up and down. I like the food, the hot dal sauce (lentil base) over rice, fried potatoes and oranges. Not much variety but fine with me. Some moleskin on a blister is the only reminder that this is new work for me.

Tonight I sleep near a buffalo again, he snores, I wonder if I do at high altitudes. I don't dream at night here or I'm not remembering dreams like I do at home. I'm finally living one of my dreams. The tension has melted away.

The message that comes to me here is one we all know well: Body, mind, earth — keep the connections strong...

Dawn. I am moving by 5 a.m. Holding a cup of tea to keep warm. It is freezing at night, but warms to a sunny 60 to 70 degrees most days. I find myself stripping down to shorts and a shirt by midday but adding a jacket and long pants when the sun drops behind a mountain for the night.

We're moving up and out of the valley now, climbing higher and higher but the elevation changes are more gradual. We will soon be above the tree line as the forest shifts to evergreens and scrub.

There are very few trekkers on the trail now, it is late in the year and we are eight days from a transportation point. We pass small groups of Tibetan nomads on horseback laughing and teasing each other. Herds of small shaggy goats trot by carrying packs followed by their kids. I sit on the ground and one tiny one comes up and nuzzles me. I cuddle him but realize I could never get this kid past customs.

The mountains around me seem closer each day; they are so high, the gorges are so deep, the cliffs so jagged, everything is exaggerated. There are a thousand Yosemite Falls tumbling down these cliffs. I am surrounded by snow and water. Rivers no one could raft, fed by glaciers, grey icy, surging around boulders as big as houses and as smooth as river-washed pebbles.

There are only pine trees now, all the tropical and midland traces are gone, tomorrow I will be above the tree line. Yet, in the middle of the trail I encounter a colony of monkeys, macques I guess. Living in a little wooded oasis, swinging, chattering and staring at me as I tiptoe by.

There are no communication links unless one climbs up to Jomosom where there is an outpost of the Nepalese army. We cook over wood fires and use candles once the sun goes down. One of the marvels I see is a grinding wheel in a little wood house straddling a waterfall. A woman serenely grinds wheat in the middle of a raging 300 foot waterfall. The stone wheel is turned by the paddles hit by the descending water.

At lunch I share my spot in the sun with two sleeping water buffalos. They are such big, lumpy creatures and chickens are sitting on them as they snore in great rumbles. The bull sounds just like my father. As kids we were so impressed with the noise he could make that we used to go into the bedroom and listen when he took a Sunday nap.

The higher we climb the more Tibetans pass us on the trail. Many are at bare survival and they beg for money or food. Some live in makeshift stone-huts that could never keep out the cold nights. These are refugees from the Chinese takeover of Tibet...

Today begins with a sandstorm. It was so severe last night it blew the tents down. I have never been in the middle of such a bitter swirling wind. I know the Himalayas test their pilgrims but what am I doing here with my shirt tied over my face to keep out the stinging sand. We are crossing a high plateau bending into a 60 mph wind, at times it blows me backward. We finally reach Jomosom hoping for an oasis and ending up with a dustbowl. A few trekkers gathered around a charcoal brazier in a house called the Om Hotel. They are waiting for the small charter plane that can land here. This is the only air strip in northwestern Nepal and the plane is unreliable because it is dependent on the winds. They have been waiting four days.

There is only scrub grass at these heights as we move on to Kagbeni, a Tibetan settlement. Yak pastures stretch everywhere. Steep hills and the ever present snow covered Himalayas. I find a faucet in the next village with some warm water heated by a solar panel on the roof. Modern or ancient technology? There has been enough sun that day and I take my first shower in a week.

The Tibetans I meet now still laugh and dance but they try to sell me silver that is not silver and stones that are made of glass. All the stashes they pull out when my white face comes into view are the same. This jewelry is made somewhere else. They know it, I know it but they are hustling to survive...

We continue on through other small settlements. I want to climb higher, to travel in the snow fields but I have neither the equipment to withstand the cold nor the courage to move any farther from contact with the outside world. When I tumbled down a short cliff today I realized that a broken bone is a disaster on these high trails. I wanted to climb all the the way to Tibet but the border is still closed and it is below zero tonight. Time to turn around, mark the spot and return to start again.

* * *

INNER RESOURCES

We all have problems but we rarely use our inner resources to solve them.

I occasionally conduct magic meetings. One is just a meeting in a meadow with an imaginary woman who is very wise. She is always available to me if I'll sit quietly and wait.

Another is a meeting of interesting people. We sit around the table and they each tell me what they would do. I invite those I think have some experience with the problem and they're always willing to share their knowledge.

Last time I invited Georgia O'Keefe, Jane Austen, Stephen Spielberg, Alice Walker, Charles Dickens and Thomas Jefferson.

Try rising above yourself with a group of friends and gain a new perspective.

Who would you invite to help?

HELP!

"The individual must control his deepest perception of himself, lest he be overwhelmed by the forces of negativism and defeatism in the weaker individuals around him."

— *Napoleon Hill*

ZOOS

What's your view of zoos? Some resent the cages, however they are contrived to seem natural. A polar bear should sit on ice, not concrete. A gorilla deserves more than just a few friends. What if the giraffe doesn't like her mate?

Others have slowly understood, with some grief, that zoos — hopefully good zoos — have become the repository for the animals of the world. Animals we cannot eat, or wear, or pet, or work will eventually run out of space. There is not room for all of us and our first commitment is to humans.

Yet adult humans appear to have a choice of circumstance and zoo animals do not. They must depend on our willingness to care for them.

The quality of our zoos is a test of our grace.

THERAPY

The therapeutic process is as misunderstood by counselors as it is by clients. A recent article by Ed Severinghaus* reminded me of the key elements:

- The therapist is healed by the patients she sees.

- The therapist lets healing happen through her.

- All problems are at root some form of guilt and inability to forgive.

- The therapist's main role is to help the client experience forgiveness by approaching him with love and without judgment.

- We all believe that we are victims of the body or of the world.

- Everyone believes at some level that to attack is salvation, it beats feeling guilty.

- We need to have tremendous respect for the power of the ego, and the tenacity with which we hold onto guilt.

- Forgiveness is the hardest thing in this world.

We must remember that most of our problems are in the mind, not in actions, or the body. It is the mind that must be healed.

* Based on a seminar by Ken Wapnick titled "Psychotherapy and the Course in Miracles."

VOCATION

Alene Moris, in her wonderful book *Uncommon Sense*, asks the question about work, "Is this all there is?" Alene answers with the allegory of the three stonemasons. Men who work at a repetitive, physically exhausting task.

"*A passerby stops and talks with each of them in turn. "What are you doing?" he asks the first one. The reply comes with irritation and fatigue: "Obviously, I am chiseling stone." The questioner walks further to the second worker and repeats the question. "What are you doing?" To which the reply is: "I'm helping construct this building." Continuing through the stoneyard, the passerby asks the third mason the same question. This time the answer is very different. The man looks up quietly: I'm building a cathedral to the glory of God.*"

Before Monday comes each one of us needs to know what we're doing and why.

BALANCE

Everything seems to speed up in the fall. Cooler weather changes our metabolism. Summer winding down changes our perception. The temptation is to speed toward Christmas, collapse and start over with the New Year.

It's time for a stress inoculation.

Assume you'll be out of breath and plan for it. Take out your calendar and set aside mini-vacations, "blobette" days (time to drop out and do nothing), afternoons of solitude, hours of silence, novels to read, massages, gentle walks, cups of herb tea, moments to choose peace.

Pleasure and productivity depend on a balance within you, set by you, for you.

GOOD AND EVIL

"If only there were evil people somewhere insidiously committing evil deeds and it were necessary only to separate them from the rest of us and destroy them. But the line dividing good and evil cuts through the heart of every human being. And who is willing to destroy a piece of his own heart?"

— *Alexander Solzhenitsyn (In the Gulag Archipelago)*

NEW AGE

There is so much misinterpretation of "new age" philosophy that I want to write about it. Many people refuse to blend the best of their past views with the best of any new view. They think one has to accept a new perspective as gospel and forsake all others. "New age" ideas are just another set of tools for coping with the universe. New tools to put with the ones you already have.

First you have to meet the basic demands of life for food, shelter and personal security, then you can check out your perspective and evaluate whether it emphasizes joy or sorrow.

It is possible to work on the real pain and problems of life while believing in and trying to live the ideal of the love between us. It is not an either or situation. I think we resist the very simplicity of the choices we have. We prefer the answers to be deeper, harder, more complex. We prefer joy wrought from pain like blood out of a stone to joy accepted as the air we breathe.

We hold on to our suffering. It is familiar, an old predictable friend. It hurts less than the pain of change.

I do not suggest you leave your forts and your usual coping tools, only that you open the windows and look at new possibilities.

Most of the wonderful steps we've taken towards a better understanding of life were once someone's crackpot dreams.

CRAP

"No one can make you feel inferior without your consent."

— *Eleanor Roosevelt*

It's not easy to decide on your value and hold on to it. Have you ever been sailing through a day and suddenly a sharp word brought you down?

We give other people tremendous power over our perspective. Even when we are at our peak, feeling clear, we allow their view to cloud our own.

Put together a perspective survival kit. You can memorize it or carry it with you — a phrase, a poem, a place, a taste, a sound, a picture, a smell, a person, a skip, a hug, a shrug, a letter, a deep breath, a warmth from another time.

If all that is too touchy-feelie for you, just remember — when people put shit in your cup — don't drink it!

EGO OR SPIRIT

The choice is always there, to build or tear down.

The ego tries to make all that surrounds us fit our comfort zone and beliefs about our value. The spirit desires to create security by giving ourselves and others acceptance.

Ego wants to blame, to stake out turf and defend it. Spirit wants to accept, forgive and work for a better future.

Your moment-to-moment contacts with life give you the opportunity to choose ego or spirit, love or fear.

A quick intake of breath, as you decide what you will be and what we are.

"Let us build the Earth by building one another."
— Pierre Teilhard de Chardin

HATRED

"The holiest of all the spots on earth is where an ancient hatred has been replaced by a present love."
— Course in Miracles

Every problem has gift for you in its hands. — R. Bach

NEPAL JOURNEY VII

I don't want to turn my back on the mountains, I have been captured. Winding down the trail is peaceful, familiar. Accustomed to the exertion, the food and the floors we sleep on, it seems easy. My guide always quiet becomes a shadow and I slip into my own thoughts.

The path down to Pokhara starts to change me as I realize I am going towards home not away from it. I slowly shift from adventurer to traveller, concerned about time and arriving on a day when it will be possible to fly to Katmandu. We cross the last valley into Pokhara, through the bazaar, across the lake on the raft and I say goodbye to Minma, the Sherpa guide and give him all the equipment and clothes I no longer need. I brought too much and there is no need to carry it back. We have hardly spoken, so have not become friends, only traveling companions...

Hot shower, sheets on the bed, dessert and a ride the next morning in a land rover to the airport. A beautiful mountain flight to Katmandu. The reality of baggage, tickets, Katmandu, dirt and too many people who must spend their life in the streets.

Katmandu is sunk in the fog when I awake but my flight to Bangkok is on time. Up through the clouds for a last glimpse of the Himalayas through the window. My neck aches from craning to see the last tooth of the jagged, incredible saw across the top of the world.

The sun at this altitude looks like a pale moon and I start thinking about home. It has been five weeks and a world away from American culture and my family. The altitude and the climb have had little effect on me. The perception of being on top of the world has. A sense of responsibility because of the options I have that others do not. It is time for a practical commitment to the rest of the world, not a philosophical one.

At the top of the world the issues of survival have little to do with questions of happiness or meaning. I can visit and thrill at the beauty of Nepal but I will return to the security and lifestyle of Seattle.

I find I'm leaving bits and pieces of myself wherever I travel. So much of me will remain in these mountains, that I sense I will return soon to climb the rest of the trail to Tibet and to reclaim this feeling and these memories...

*   *   *

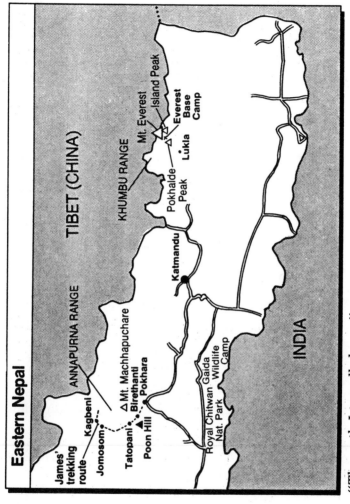

Eastern Nepal

TIBET (CHINA)

ANNAPURNA RANGE

KHUMBU RANGE

James'
trekking
route

Kagbeni

Jomosom

Tatopani
Birethanti
Poon Hill

△ Mt. Machhapuchare

Pokhara

Royal Chitwan Gaida
Wildlife
Nat. Park Camp

Katmandu

Pokhalde
Peak

Mt. Everest

Island Peak

Everest
Base
Camp

Lukla

INDIA

"The path I travelled on..."

115

HOLIDAYS

Holiday time is here: the challenge to treat each other with grace and remember the importance of the connections between us.

It isn't easy so here are a few rules for relatives:

- Take very good care of yourself so you aren't stressed out and crabby.
- Don't expect or attempt perfection; settle for anything short of a disaster.
- Don't ask if the pies are homemade.
- Don't correct or criticize anyone.
- Choose to be happy, not right.
- Don't care who gets the credit for whatever.
- Avoid competition and comparison; don't keep score.
- Give up playing martyr or victim.
- When in doubt, keep quiet.
- Remember, very few things are truly important.

Then thank everyone for staying alive so you can love or hate them for another year. Your relatives may not be perfect, but they are yours.

CHRISTMAS

Christmas can seem overwhelming if you miss the gift it promises. The holidays offer a rebirth of spirit at the coldest season of the year, the winter before the spring.

You are asked to see and hear the beauty all around, the love within. Christmas is a time to move closer to each other, generate warmth, celebrate life.

There is only one thing that can stop the Christmas spirit: the speed at which you travel through the season.

The music is there if you take the time to listen. The spirit is there if you take the time to let it touch your heart. The beauty is there if you give yourself time to see.

The commercialization of Christmas is an injection of speed that you can bypass. Walk slower, feel more, do less. You can have the spirit for nothing more than your time.

Give yourself time for Christmas.

NEW YEAR

I've just returned from five weeks away, most of it spent trekking in the Himalayas with a guide.

There was no great spiritual breakthrough. I learned my body is strong, simplicity is a form of peace, the joy of solitude and the incredible beauty of the "top of the world."

I met people who live very close to the earth and the living things around them. Some nights I slept near chickens and water buffaloes. The stars were so close and so bright that I felt I could touch them.

The pleasure of climbing up mountains carrying one's home, traveling light, feeling the energy, the freedom, the exhilaration.

I kept a promise that I made at the beginning of last year: to go to Nepal. I now know I will return someday to climb higher and farther.

But now the year is slipping away and this is the time to think about the promise of the New Year, not just the pleasures of the old.

What is your agenda for the New Year?

Stop a moment and think about the possibilities that stretch before you.

My agenda was formed in the high country but it is hard to articulate.

Robert Pirsig has also traveled in mountains, and he writes in "Zen and the Art of Motorcycle Maintenance" more clearly what I am trying to form as a resolution:

"I want to talk about another high country now in the world of thought... the high country of the mind...

"Few people travel here. There's no real profit to be made from wandering through it, yet like this high country of the material world around us, it has its own austere beauty that to some people make the hardships of traveling through it worthwhile.

"In the high country of the mind, one has to become adjusted to the thinner air of uncertainty..."

It's time for me to stay closer to home, take risks, write about more private journeys and give on a more practical level. Working on hunger and basic medical care brings one closer to the earth than philosophical questions about meaning. Sharing food and shelter with Nepalese and Tibetans changes priorities.

There is a balance between survival and philosophy. As Peter Matthiessen writes in "The Snow Leopard," the great sins according to the Sherpas are to pick wildflowers and to threaten children.

It's time to escape the public presence and measure the choices within my own lifespan. It's time that I learned to be mortal.

Mortality is all around us as we recap the events of another year and buy new calendars. We avoid thinking about how many New Years we have left.

Listening to the recap of important deaths in the last year, we miss the rebirth promised with the acceptance of our own death. The acceptance of mortality that makes life more precious.

How much time do you have left? And how do you want to spend it?

For the New Year, draw a time line on a piece of paper. Put the year of your birth on one end, then each year until 1985. Choose a hypothetical year of death.

1943	**1985**	**2025**

What do you have time for?....................

. . . .
. . . .
. . . .
. . . .
. . . .

What do you want to stop wasting time on?......

. . . .
. . . .
. . . .
. . . .
. . . .

What would you do if you only had a year? ......

. . . .
. . . .
. . . .
. . . .
. . . .

Learn to be mortal as a guide for your life. Weigh your choices against the time clock. What are your priorities? What is truly important? What do you want? Do you have time to be abusive or to be abused? What do you have time to care about or give to yourself and your world?

Learning to be mortal is our guide for living.

"Every moment of life is to be lived calmly, mindfully, as if it were the last, to ensure that the most is made of the precious human state," Matthiessen writes in "The Snow Leopard."

We are all in this life together. What you choose affects us all.

Along all the paths I traveled these past weeks, I was greeted, even by small children, with hands together as in prayer, head gently bowed and the word *namaste*. The greeting translates as "I salute the God within you."

Namaste — friends, readers, travelers: Remember the Spirit within you and between us as another year unfolds.

The holiest spot on Earth is where an ancient hatred is *replaced* by a present love.

*Remember to take
good care of yourself.*

Other Books by Jennifer James Ph.D.

SUCCESS IS THE QUALITY OF YOUR JOURNEY.
This book is a selection of Jennifer's commentaries. There are over 100 witty, thoughtful and sometimes moving selections that will add optimism and depth to your life. $5.95

LIFE IS A GAME OF CHOICE. The book is made up of twenty-six pages of information with illustrations on how you can find out what you want and make changes in your life. $2.95

THE SLUG MANUAL: THE RISE AND FALL OF CRITICISM. This 92-page illustrated book is a collection of comments and information on how to handle criticism. It is humorous and very helpful if you find yourself, or someone you care about, sensitive to criticism. $4.25

Tapes Available:

- **DIRECTIONS FOR CHANGE: EXCELLENCE AND OPTIMISM**
- **SELF-ESTEEM**
- **MANAGING STRESS**
- **PARENTING SKILLS**
- **FAMILY SELF-ESTEEM**
- **SUCCESS IN RELATIONSHIPS**
- **PERFECTIONISM AND SELF-WORTH**
- **ZEST FOR LIFE** (Two tapes: $15.00)
- **CRITICISM**
- **WHEN YOUR PARENTS GROW OLD**
- **BEING SINGLE: CHANGE AND RISK**

Tapes - $9.95 each, including postage

Special discounts are available for counselors, teachers and non-profit organizations.

All prices include shipping and handling. Send check or money order to: Jennifer James Inc., 3903 E. James, Seattle, WA 98122